"Me" Time

Discover How Great You Are

Written and illustrated by
Shannon Braybrook

FriesenPress

Suite 300 - 990 Fort St
Victoria, BC, V8V 3K2
Canada

www.friesenpress.com

ISBN
978-1-5255-7113-8 (Hardcover)
978-1-5255-7114-5 (Paperback)
978-1-5255-7115-2 (eBook)

1. SELF-HELP, CREATIVITY

Distributed to the trade by The Ingram Book Company

HAVE A

Beautiful DAY

FUN activities to RECHARGE YOU!!

This Book Belongs To:
_____

Dedications

I couldn't have done this without a few key people.

To my man, Dave. Thank you for believing in me and teaching me how to ride a Harley.

Let's ride into happiness, baby.

To my children, Kelsey, Nicholas, Kyndree and Quinn. Thank you for inspiring me and letting me cook for you and fifteen other kids every weekend. I love you guys.

To my dad. Thank you for teaching me how to draw eyeballs. I miss you, your attention to details, your constructive criticism and that sense of humor. This is for you, dad

To my mom. Thank you for empowering me at such a young age. Thank you for teaching me how to read a recipe, how to sew absolutely anything and how to laugh until I pee. I love you.

Thank you to Brad, Karen, Adam and Steven, my supportive brother and his family. You guys are amazing.

I have so much gratitude for my good friends and the many friends I have not yet met. Thanks for the love.

Namaste to you all,

Shannon

Introduction

I'm a healthcare worker and one morning, I was having a coffee break on shift and decided to do a small motivational activity page I found online. It asked interesting questions that made me think of my life from a different perspective. One of the questions was if I was happy in my life and what I did every day to keep myself motivated. This lit a little spark under me.

I asked my colleagues if any of them were interested in filling out one of the pages as well. Pretty soon I was seeing finished pages lying all around the office. It made me happy to know I had suggested something new and uplifting for my team to try. Most of them enjoyed the activity and that prompted me to bring art supplies, canvases and paints to work so the staff as well as the clients could partake in a painting party!

I began asking others around me what motivated them in life and what kinds of things they liked to do for fun. The most common answer was usually that they liked watching TV or surfing the net. I felt like people were really burning out and losing touch with themselves and their own bliss.

This book is about taking a journey of discovery; it's about discovering yourself and what makes you happy. It asks questions that make you think about your life and if you are living it in the best way possible. It is meant to help you build self-confidence so you can get through daily challenges.

I have compiled my favorite exercises in one handy book, including fun projects like vision boards and gratitude journals, . I am proud of what you are holding in your hands right now. I chose to illustrate the book myself as a way to personalize it even more. I've gathered a diverse cross section of information, activities and questions about self-discovery helping to invoke positive changes in your life.

When was the last time you checked in with yourself to see how you were doing? Are you living your most perfect life? In this little workbook, I show you how to meditate your way to peacefulness and how to focus and practice mindfulness with coloring, puzzles and challenges. You can even create some mouth watering treats! The exercises in this book are meant to inspire you, motivate you and recharge you. I hope you get as much from this book as I did from writing it. I wish you a wonderful journey on your road to self-awareness. Go out and live your best life.

Safety First

The safety of individuals using this book is of the utmost importance to me. Please use caution when out collecting on nature/city walks. Stay to the trails and obey important signs. When trying a new exercise or deep breathing, consult with your doctor to make sure you are good to go. Most ingredients in my recipes can be substituted with desired alternatives. Please assist inexperienced chefs in the kitchen when using knives or the stove. Safety first. Have fun!

Vacation Word Seek
top to bottom, left to right

destination
luggage
sunshine
train

plane
travel
reservation
voyage

layover
passport
red-eye
bathing suit

cabin
tickets
beach

cruise
hotel
tourist

d	b	a	t	h	i	n	g	s	u	i	t	r
e	e	a	r	s	u	c	r	u	i	s	e	e
s	a	b	a	q	p	l	a	n	e	l	t	s
t	c	p	v	c	d	w	e	s	g	u	o	e
i	h	r	e	d	e	y	e	h	f	g	u	r
n	n	o	l	x	c	a	b	i	n	g	r	v
a	t	i	c	k	e	t	s	n	t	a	i	a
t	l	a	y	o	v	e	r	e	r	g	s	t
i	v	o	y	a	g	e	e	t	a	e	t	i
o	p	a	s	s	p	o	r	t	i	h	i	o
n	g	h	o	t	e	l	k	l	n	m	j	n

Dreaming Word Seek
top to bottom, left to right

cabin money fame happy health
courage bravery relax farm family
love education vacation hammock forest
garden mansion plane imagine car

h e a l t h t a z f a r m
a g s h r f q i p y h p x
m a n s i o n o m j a l k
m h g f m r b n v w n a l
o e a a a e r c a b i n c
c a r m g s a m c r h e o
k l d i i t v u a e a o u
f t e l n r e w t l p s r
a h n y e x r v i a p g a
m o n e y q y p o x y w g
e d u c a t i o n l o v e

SHANNON BRAYBROOK

Awakening Word Seek
top to bottom, left to right

dignity
epiphany
accepting
tranquil

welcoming
respect
content
spiritual

observing
embracing
laughter
appreciative

ethereal
wonder
love

harmonious
noble
joy

```
s  r  h  a  r  m  o  n  i  o  u  s
e  e  m  b  r  a  c  i  n  g  w  n
y  s  p  i  r  i  t  u  a  l  n  o
e  p  i  p  h  a  n  y  m  g  x  b
t  e  w  e  l  c  o  m  i  n  g  l
h  c  w  o  n  d  e  r  t  d  n  e
e  t  r  n  a  q  u  i  l  i  v  l
r  o  b  s  e  r  v  i  n  g  z  o
e  b  a  c  c  e  p  t  i  n  g  v
a  p  p  r  e  c  i  a  t  i  v  e
l  a  u  g  h  t  e  r  x  t  s  w
c  o  n  t  e  n  t  j  o  y  r  t
```

GRATITUDE

"The more grateful I am, the more beauty I see."
Mary Davis

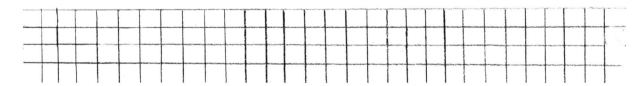

CHAPTER 1
Gratitude

Daily Affirmation: I am so grateful. I choose to be thankful no matter my circumstances.

The definition of gratitude is to have thanks and appreciation. It stems from the Latin word *gratus*, which means thankful and pleasing. Gratitude puts us into a better state of mind. It creates positive emotions in us and others. It is important for keeping the whole body, mind and soul strong and healthy.

Gratitude Exercise

I believe a thankful heart is a happy heart. When we have gratitude for what we already have, it tells the universe to keep sending more great stuff our way. This project can be a fun reminder to stay thankful each and every day.

To get started, draw a large heart on a piece of paper. Divide the heart into sections. In each section, draw or describe in words something that you are thankful for. Add more sections if you need to. You can give thanks for absolutely anything that is important to you. This is for your eyes only. If you give daily thanks for all the things you have in life, this action alone is enough to elevate your mood and make you happier.

Questions to Ponder

If you could thank five people for their positive contributions to your life, who would they be and what did they do to make your life a little better? It can be anyone: a historical figure, a family member, a teacher. If they are alive, go say thank you. If they are not, just say it aloud. Put it out into the universe—they might get the message.

Cool Idea

You've spent some time on the topic of gratitude and why it is important to express it. . Why not create your very own personalized gratitude journal? It will be a special place for you to record your thoughts and feelings of thankfulness every day. You can draw, paint, write or collage on each page. This is just for your eyes, so have fun with it. Enjoy the process of gratitude.

To create a gratitude journal, you can:

1. Purchase a book with blank pages

2. Create your own book by using heavy paper for the cover and filling it with blank or lined paper. You can hole punch and use ribbon to attach it or staple it together on one side and it's ready to write in!

Thoughts on Gratitude

Did you know that practicing gratitude on a daily basis helps keep you present, will elevate your mood, can give you a deeper perspective of life and generally just makes you a happier person? Taking time out of every day to be thankful for what you have is a wonderful way to practice gratitude. It is important to say thank you for each small thing that we receive. Maybe you want to say thank you to the sun for shining or to a bird for cheering you up with a song. When you have fresh water or a warm meal to eat, be thankful. Everything is a gift from our universe (or God, or Creator or Consciousness). Do you have a roof over your head? A great job? A new love? New great health? Whatever it is, say thank you. You will receive more of what you already appreciate.

☐	Daily Affirmation
☐	Daily Meditation
☐	Move in nature
☐	Collect for Project

SELF CONFIDENCE

"Don't be satisfied with stories, how things have gone with others. Unfold your own myth."
Rumi

CHAPTER 2
Self-Confidence

Daily Affirmation: I am worthy of all the good things that happen in my life. I have confidence and the strength to do anything I set my mind to.

The definition of self-confidence is the feeling of trust in one's abilities, qualities and one's own judgment.

Self-Confidence Exercise

You know that little voice inside of your head? The one that can sometimes be extremely judgmental? Well, this voice can also be sweet and kind; it just takes practice. When you learn to be your own cheerleader and speak lovingly to yourself, you can get through any situation in life. This project is a reinforcement of positive words directed to yourself: a visual cue to remind you of your own value and abilities.

Confidence and Posture

Remember that your powerful stance shows self-confidence and control. Having great posture matters! Looking your best, dressing for success and projecting self-confidence helps you in every aspect of life; especially when job searching, doing interviews, promoting yourself or public speaking. It really makes a difference in how you feel as well: just the act of standing up tall increases testosterone and brain power, as well as lowering cortisol so you can feel less stressed.

The best way to improve posture is to practice. Stand with your shoulders dropped and back, chin tucked in a bit and eyes forward. Do this in front of the mirror for a few minutes each morning. This daily check-in will start you off on the right foot to move with confidence in everything you do. How does it feel to stand tall? Do you feel more confident?

Project 1

Trace both of your hands onto a piece of paper. Write or draw a positive thing about yourself in each of the fingers of the hands. In the center (palm), fill in the blanks:

- ▷ I am _____.
- ▷ I can_____.
- ▷ I will _____.

Color, draw, paint or embellish the hands with glitter or special treasures you have found. Hang this up to remind you of all your positive attributes. These words will help build self-esteem and confidence. You've got this!

Project 2

Here are a few ideas to help build confidence before any event, such as an exam or an interview. Try any of these relaxing suggestions to calm nerves and help you get through that next big thing with ease.

- ▷ Stand tall in front of the mirror for a few moments. Say your affirmations.
- ▷ Take a warm bubble bath. You can add Epsom salts for magnesium, which increases serotonin in the brain thus relaxing your body and mind.
- ▷ Try deep breathing – five or ten minutes will reduce heart rate and calm nerves.
- ▷ Take a brisk walk.
- ▷ Unwind with a cup of tea. Chamomile or peppermint are relaxing.
- ▷ Sigh. It releases CO_2 to reduce tension.
- ▷ Create a task list before an event (to keep surprises at a minimum).

Questions to Ponder

Changing your inner dialogue from negative to positive words and thoughts can have a profound impact on your life and your self-confidence. Speak to your own self as though you were speaking to a best friend or a small child. Kindness and loving words should be the goal. Make a list of ten positive and uplifting sentences that describe you, such as "I am a fantastic artist."

Something to think about

I think so many of us could use a little boost of confidence and motivation during our day. One very easy way to obtain this is to practice self-awareness exercises in front of a mirror and spend some quality time each day saying nice things to ourselves. A few years ago, I started writing on my bathroom mirror with a dry-erase marker. I draw happy faces and fun quotes around the border, and it always makes me focus for a minute on my present moment and how I feel. The whole family benefits from reading these loving quotes every morning. If you read it, say it, and think it, you will be it.

A Helping Hand

Often, we spend so much time focusing on ourselves and our busy lives that we forget the type of positive impact we can have on others on a daily basis. Can you think of a few times where you made a difference in someone else's life? Do you stop by your grandma's to have tea and listen to stories? Maybe you helped out a friend when she needed some daycare for her kids? Doing things for others, when you can, will build bonds and create trust. Lend a helping hand and see how good you feel afterwards.

☐	Daily Affirmation
☐	Daily Meditation
☐	Move In Nature
☐	Collect for Project

SHANNON BRAYBROOK

SELF-DETERMINATION

"The willingness to show up changes us. It makes us a little braver each time."
Brené Brown

CHAPTER 3
Self-Determination

Daily Affirmation: I have self-control. I will make good choices today. I am determined to succeed.

Self-determination is a combination of self-control, decision making and regulating one's own behavior. The area of the brain responsible for self-determination is the prefrontal cortex, which can be exercised and strengthened by doing "neuroplasticity" exercises like the ones included in this chapter. The term "neuroplasticity" means the ability of the brain to form and reorganize synaptic connections, especially in response to learning or following injury. In other words, you can build your brain like any other muscle.

Self-Determination Exercise

This exercise is meant to help us break habits that no longer serve us in a positive way. We all want to be fit and healthy but sometimes things can hold us back from making choices that benefit our bodies and minds.

Building self-determination and self-control will improve so many areas of your life. Being able to say no to something you really crave is difficult but not impossible. Remember that old habits are hard to break, so give yourself plenty of time to adjust to your new ways. Have patience in the process, and continue to move towards a healthier and happier life by removing one unwanted habit at a time. Oh, and by the way, you've got this.

Project

Create some cue cards as a visual aid to help change habits (any habit, as simple as nail-biting or as complex as quitting smoking). Cut out a paper square for each habit you would like to work on. Write one habit per card. Turn the card over and write three to five things you are willing to do to change or remove this habit. Keep the cards handy as a reminder of your self-determination and willingness to make positive change.

Questions to Ponder

Do you have a difficult area of your life where you could benefit from having more self- control? Does this area cause you unnecessary stress and frustration? Would you like to work on gaining control of this situation as well as every other one you come upon?

Think of one or two things you can do to start gaining more control of this stressful area of your life. Here is an example: You would like to start going to bed earlier, as heading to bed in the early morning hours is effecting your productivity at work. Making some small changes to your nightly routine, like soaking in a warm bath, doing deep-breathing exercises, drinking a hot cup of chamomile tea or listening to soothing music s will gradually make it easier to get to bed at a more appropriate time.

Note: If you experience chronic difficulties with sleep, see your doctor to determine if there is any other reason for the insomnia.

Cool Idea

If you have an extreme sweet tooth, do not deprive yourself of treats—just decrease their quantity and frequency. I love chocolate, and it can really affect me when I don't have some. Each week during my trip to the grocery store, I buy one or two treats from the bulk food section, such as a small amount of chocolate like bridge mix or Smarties. It usually works out to be less than one regular chocolate bar. I have cut back to maybe a quarter of my usual sugary habit, and it feels pretty good. Why not give it a try? You don't have to eliminate the things you love, just cut back a bit.

Interesting Stuff

Meditation has a host of positive health benefits. Calming the body, resting the mind and concentrating on breath helps keep you grounded and focused. Did you know that just ten minutes of meditation gives the fastest results of all self-determination exercises? One basic way to meditate is to sit or lie in a comfortable position, close your eyes and breathe naturally. Focus on your breathing but do not try to control it. Do this for a few minutes before any type of challenge in your day. Breathe in the good, breathe out the gratitude.

☐	Daily Affirmation
☐	Daily Meditation
☐	Move In Nature
☐	Collect for Project

MOTIVATION

"Only I can change my life. No one can do it for me."
Carol Burnett
"Greatness and madness are next-door neighbors and they often borrow each other's sugar."
Joe Rogan

CHAPTER 4
Motivation

Daily Affirmation: I am my own cheerleader. I know my worth. I can do anything I set my mind to.

Motivation is the general desire or willingness to do something. Without motivation it is difficult to start anything.

Do you remember one time in your life when your motivation was so strong that you overcame something really difficult, scary or overwhelming without even thinking about it?

Project

This exercise uses a goal-setting worksheet to help you organize goals in order, keeping a time frame in mind. Take a clean piece of paper and across the top put three headings:

- ▷ Thirty-day goal
- ▷ One-year goal
- ▷ Five-year goal

Under each time frame, write a goal that you want to attain. It may be financial, career orientated or maybe a vacation plan. Under the goal, write the first five steps you will take towards making it happen. Stay motivated by checking back and adding steps to your worksheet.

Here is an example under the five-year goal "**buying a home**."

Here are five steps to get started

1. Create a savings account.
2. Decide your house price range and begin searching real estate listings
3. Look at ways to increase income to help with down payment

4. Look at ways to decrease debt and credit cards to ease that monthly mortgage
5. Visualize that new home and you living in it.

The ways you get to the goal are your own choice. Do what you need to do to stay motivated and focused; you can do anything you put your mind to. Researching every aspect of your goal also takes any surprises out of the picture, ie: property taxes, interest rates, cost to commute etc.

Questions to Ponder

In your daily life at work or at home, how do you keep yourself motivated? Do you ever have challenges with unmotivated family or work colleagues? What do you do to motivate others? Does one thing stand out as being the best motivator for your team?

Cool Idea

Let's keep this positive momentum going; every little step forward is a step forward. Broken down into bits, a goal can be attained without being so intimidating. For this exercise, write out one or two goals you would like to achieve this week (try a short-term goal first and work towards the longer ones). Think about it for a minute then write down the first step for each goal. Every time you complete a step, write another and complete it. Enjoy the feeling of completing each task and getting closer to your goal. Don't worry if the goal takes longer than a week to attain. Keep moving towards it at your own pace until it is done.

Interesting Stuff

Did you know that the brain's frontal lobe is in control of your motivation? One fun way to develop this area is to practice juggling. The reason juggling is a great brain builder is because of the way your neurons speed up to fire more rapidly as you learn to move three balls in sync. This action increases your focus, vision, memory and movement. Also, juggling is just plain fun! This instructional video from Howcast has clear direction and great visuals: https://www.howcast.com/videos/944-how-to-juggle-three-balls

☐	Daily Affirmation
☐	Daily Meditation
☐	Move in Nature
☐	Collect for Project

MANIFESTATION

"You are the author of your life. If you don't like how it goes, write it differently."
Iva Kenaz

CHAPTER 5
Manifestation

Daily Affirmation: My mind is clear and focused. I am making my dreams come true by putting attention on them.

Manifestation, in the context of attraction, is something that appears into your physical reality through thought, feelings and beliefs. This means that whatever you focus on is what you are bringing into your reality.

Manifestation Exercise

Are there things you would like to attract into your life? One of my favorite tools for attracting stuff is a vision board I create at least once a year. It outlines in detail what my husband and I want in that year. We use felt pens on a poster board, and I am addicted to sketching, so whatever we want to manifest into our lives gets drawn on the board.

It is so much fun ticking things off as they happen. It may seem a little strange, but when you focus and see a goal so often, you start to work towards achieving that goal. The universe around you lines things up. We know action is necessary, so we work hard to stay on the path that gets us to where we want to be. We are also constantly adding things we want to the board. We never remove anything. It feels like if it's important enough to put on there, we should do our best to attract those things into our world.

Questions to Ponder

Do you have difficulty saving money? Is it hard to just leave it in a jar or an envelope without wanting to sneak from it? I came up with a fun way to stay constantly reminded about what you are saving for so maybe sneaking cash won't be your goal: saving cash will.

Grab some acrylic paints, brushes, a container like a glass jar, a used flat wallet or a wooden box with a lid. Decide what you would like to save money for; it can be anything. Go ahead and paint the item you are saving for directly onto the wallet, glass container or box. Do your best to make it look like what you want, and it doesn't have to be perfect. It could be a car, or maybe you need a new dishwasher. The idea is to store money in this container until you have enough to purchase what is painted on the outside. Every time you look at the painting and container, you will be reminded that the money inside is going towards something really important and that it is possible to save for what you want. Good luck, and have fun making that next purchase with cash!

Cool Idea

Create mini dream cards, which are a smaller version of your vision poster. Cut three-inch squares from heavy card stock or use blank recipe cards. On the back of each card, draw or write what you want in your life. Be specific and detailed. Instead of writing the word "vehicle," describe the make, model and color. If you want a promotion, specify in which area of the business. Be thoughtful as you write each word; your intention is to manifest it into your reality. Really elaborate on what you desire. On the back of each card, use one word only to be your affirmation word, and say it. For example, it could be "promotion."

Once you put the thought out into the universe of you getting that promotion, things just start lining up. For example, you may get that all-important phone call or praise at your job. This is moving you towards your desire. Scientists are more and more interested these days in things like manifestation, group mindfulness and how exercising the brain is beneficial and possible. Use your little dream cards as inspirational reminders to put the work in, focus on the goal and go get what you want. Remember to be thankful for what you have but grateful also for what is in store. I am wishing you abundance, love, joy and bliss.

Interesting Stuff

This is a great article from Shelly Bullard, MFT, Marriage and Family Therapist, talking about the five practical ways to manifest love into your life. It is very informative, and I suggest digging deeper and checking out her original article at https://www.mindbodygreen.com/0-15377/5-practical-ways-to-manifest-love-seriously.html

I appreciate that this is a practical application and that it does work.

5 practical ways to start creating an amazing relationship

1. Claim what you want

2. Be whatever you want to create more of

3. Get clear on the type of partner you want to be with

4. Love yourself

5. Relax, trust and enjoy this awesome life

☐	Daily Affirmation
☐	Daily Meditation
☐	Move In Nature
☐	Collect for Project

Chapter 6

MY healthy BODY

HEALTHY BODY

"The first wealth is health."
Ralph Waldo Emerson
"Don't eat anything your great grandmother wouldn't recognize as food."
Michael Pollan

CHAPTER 6
Healthy Body

Daily Affirmation: I appreciate and love my body. Every cell is working to keep me alive.

A healthy body refers to the state of emotional and physical well-being. Factors for good health include genetics, relationships, your environment and education. You can enhance your own personal health by including healthy foods into your diet, a regular exercise regimen, and proactive screening for disease.

Healthy Body Exercise

Before starting any new physical activity, make sure you know your limits. Dress comfortably, stay hydrated, stretch a little, take a few deep breaths, and if possible, turn off the phone (or turn it to vibrate).

Now, let's do a little dancing! You can dance with headphones or without. If you work at an office job, you can chair dance by moving your upper body to the beat. After dinner, when the kids are ready for bed, why not have a little dance party to burn up excess energy? It doesn't matter what type of moving you do, just move! After a few songs, you will feel so invigorated and full of positive energy.

Questions to Ponder

How will you fit more movement into your day? What type of exercise do you feel like adding to your life? The gym, kayaking, walking in the park? You can change things up each day so you don't get bored of one activity. If you need a friend to inspire you, why not invite someone to go walking at the mall or around the recreation center walking track? All it takes is that first step to creating a healthy body and mind.

Cool Idea

When was the last time you jumped rope? Hula hooped? Bounced on a trampoline? If you enjoy dancing, then why not try a different form of exercise? Think outside the box. There's belly dancing, pole dancing, and even tightrope walking. There are classes for all types of exercise in every town. If you would like to work out in private and if you have the room, why not create a small workout center with a few light weights and a yoga mat for stretching in your spare room? What a perfect way to get started on a regular exercise routine. If you have children, you can set up a workout area for them as well. How about a game of Twister with the kids? Or take a brisk walk through your town or out in the forest to get the blood flowing. While you are out, make sure to collect little treasures for the chime/mobile project in Chapter 7.

Interesting Stuff

Did you know that serotonin, a hormone neurotransmitter, contributes to your well-being and happiness? Serotonin can be increased by sunlight and is very beneficial to good health. It helps keep you calm, positive and engaged or focused for longer. Why not spend some time in the sunshine today? Walk on a beach, play tennis, hike or bike. Enjoy the warmth of the sun while also increasing your happy chemical.

Did you know that getting a great night's sleep has many, many positive health benefits? With adequate sleep (especially deep sleep), the body repairs and heals blood vessels by releasing helpful hormones and by controlling the amount of energy used during sleeping hours so the body can repair. Sleep also clears waste from the brain, supporting memory and learning. Deep sleep aids us in regulating our moods, our libido and even our appetite. Before bed, try things that help you fall asleep, like herbal tea, a hot water bottle or a good book. Sweet dreams.

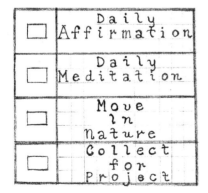

☐	Daily Affirmation
☐	Daily Meditation
☐	Move in nature
☐	Collect for Project

MINDFULNESS

"The present moment is filled with joy and happiness. If you are attentive you will see it."
Thich Nhat Hanh

CHAPTER 7
Mindfulness

Daily Affirmation: Today I inhale the positive and exhale the gratitude. I will stay present and focused.

The definition of mindfulness is the psychological process of purposely bringing one's attention to experiences occurring in the present moment without judgment; which can be developed through the practice of meditation and other training.

Mindfulness Exercise

The purpose of this exercise is for you to take a moment out of your hectic life to sit quietly and create something beautiful with your own hands. This is a chance to be mindful and present in the process as you enjoy your collection of treasures from your city/nature walks and create a beautiful handmade mobile.

You have probably seen many mobiles in your travels, but in case you haven't, a mobile is a decorative structure that is suspended so as to turn freely in air. I have included an illustration of chimes using driftwood, copper wire, quartz rocks and feathers. If you can attach it to a piece of wire, it can be hung on a mobile. If using wood, I recommend using small eye screws to attach the wire. These look nice and come in silver or gold. They are tiny and you can buy larger ones if your items are heavy or bulky. Anything goes with your mobile: chimes and bells can be added at the bottom for even more flair and a wonderful sound.

Hang your mobile/chime in a sunny spot where you can enjoy it for years to come. If you have enough treasures handy, why not make a second one as a gift? What a thoughtful present. Did it feel good working with your hands? I find it inspires me to do more when I see the finished product.

Questions to Ponder

Looking back at your day today, what was the most interesting thing you saw? The most hilarious? The most colorful? It isn't really about the seeing as much as the *being* in the moment of seeing. When we sit and just allow life to happen around us and don't engage in the acts, it frees us to just be and not interact with the happening. We don't have to judge or make a decision—just watch it unfold. Life gets really interesting when you practice mindfulness.

Cool Idea

With the rise of cell phones, computers at work and at home, online education, gaming and social media, there really isn't a quiet minute in most people's lives. Do you need a break? A little you time? How about taking a minute for mindfulness? It really is *that* easy. It takes just sixty seconds of focus to make an impact on your state of being.

I have dealt with this firsthand being a new motorcycle rider. The first minute I am sitting on my bike is very important. I take that time to breathe deeply and focus on where I am: on a motorcycle! I need to be alert.

Here are a few tips for creating a minute of mindfulness:

▷ Sixty seconds of deep breathing—inhale, hold, exhale and hold. Repeat.

▷ Hold a pose for sixty seconds. This is great for balance, memory and firing neurons. Close your eyes and visualize something you love. Open your eyes. Take a breath

Interesting Stuff

Did you know that mindfulness can be practiced on a large scale? People are starting to realize the benefits to being in large groups in silence or practicing mindfulness exercises together. There are a few really interesting things happening in group mindfulness; I have discovered things like mindful eating and mindful communication, among others. If you want to dive deeper into group mindfulness, I recommend the website www.the-reflective-mind.com. Have a look in your town to see if there are any groups getting together to do meditation, mindfulness or even yoga. Better yet, create your own group and sit together in nature or in a quiet park and be mindful together.

☐	Daily Affirmation
☐	Daily Meditation
☐	Move in nature
☐	Collect for Project

RECIPES

"Food is symbolic of love when words are inadequate."
Alan D Wolfelt

SHANNON BRAYBROOK

CHAPTER 8
Recipes

Daily Affirmation: I thoroughly enjoy new challenges in the kitchen. I love creating delicious treats for my friends and family.

Warning! These are not diet recipes. They contain butter, sugar and salt. They are indulgent, mouth-watering, rich and delicious treats to make for lunches, special occasions or to give as gifts. I love cookie exchanges, so I have included two yummy cookie recipes.

I grew up in a home where both my parents cooked, and they did it very well! My mom was a pro at comfort foods and baking. Dad was a great hunter and butcher. We were lucky enough to enjoy an entire turkey dinner cooked on a wood stove every Christmas. My brother and I were subjected to the most wonderful smells of fresh bread and pots of chicken soup. I spent so much time cooking in the kitchen with my parents that over the years I have been able to replicate many of the recipes from my childhood. I love passing down skills to my kids whenever I get the chance. Feeling confident in the kitchen just takes practice. Enjoy learning some basic cooking skills in these recipes.

Questions to Ponder

▷ Did you know that July 25 is national hot fudge sundae day? The hot fudge sundae was created at CC Browns, a Los Angeles ice cream parlor, in 1906. The original sundae resulted when Chester Platt, a druggist in 1892, tried to trademark the name "Sunday" for his cherry syrup and ice cream combination, but it was turned down and "sundae" is now used.

▷ Did you know that the vitamin-and-nutrient-rich cashew grows on a tree? The part that we eat hangs from a small fruit. Cashews contain the "good" fats that aid in the prevention of heart disease and stroke. Cashews can help in weight loss; a small amount as a snack can make you feel full.

▷ Did you know that blueberries are full of calcium, magnesium, phosphorus, iron, zinc and a few other amazing vitamins and minerals? Not only are blueberries delicious, but they are incredibly beneficial in lowering blood pressure and managing diabetes. Half a cup of berries contains three grams of fiber and 25% of your daily vitamin C.

▷ Did you know that the cakes of ancient times consisted more of nuts and dried fruits? The standard white cake became popular during the fifteenth century in Germany, and cake was no longer just for weddings. The birthday cake took its current form in the seventeenth century.

Chocolate Sundae Sauce
~So much chocolate~
makes over 2 cups

2 cups sugar dissolved in 4 cups water
4 squares unsweetened chocolate
pinch of salt
2 tbsp cornstarch and 1 tbsp cold water
2 tsp vanilla

Method

Boil sugar and water for 5 minutes to make a syrup. Add chocolate, salt and cornstarch/water mixture. Use a double boiler or heat slowly over direct heat and stir until chocolate is melted and mixture is smooth (6-9 minutes). Try not to overcook. Cool. Add vanilla. Mix well. Store in a jar in the fridge. You can warm up the entire jar in hot water or microwave for 10 seconds at a time. Stir.

Let's Make Sundaes!!

All you need is ice cream, fruit, marshmallows, sprinkles, bananas, chocolate chips, Chocolate Sundae Sauce, coconut—you name it! To create the perfect sundae, use your favorite ice cream or alternative, and scoop into bowl. Top with anything you like. Try whipped cream, chocolate sauce, sliced bananas, fresh strawberries and a cherry on top. You can alternate any ingredient with appropriate things for you and your family. We like to use frozen yogurt in place of ice cream. Challenge the family to see who can create the tastiest combinations. Why not pull out a board game and make it a party!

Fluffy White Cake
preheat oven to 400°F
grease 8 x 8 pan

2 eggs
1 cup sugar
1 cup flour
1 tsp baking powder
½ cup milk
1 tbsp butter
¼ tsp vanilla

Method

Grease an 8 x 8 pan. Beat eggs well, add sugar. Add flour and baking powder. This mixture will be really thick. Scald milk and butter in saucepan. Pour over batter and mix well. Add vanilla. Mix well. Pour batter into greased pan. Bake for 30 minutes. If you slide a toothpick into the center and it comes out clean, the cake is done. Cool. Frost with your favorite icing.

SHANNON BRAYBROOK

Candy-Coated Cashews
Makes a great gift
Sweet and spicy

2 cups sugar
½ cup water
1 lb raw cashews
1 tsp cinnamon
dash of salt

Method

Boil sugar and water until thick and clear. Add cashews. Stir with wooden spoon until the nuts make a crackling sound. Reduce heat. Stir until dry. Remove nuts and add enough water to moisten the sugar in the pan. Add cinnamon and salt and boil until syrup spins thread on the spoon, 230°F on candy thermometer. Add nuts back into pan and stir until thoroughly coated and separated. Keep heat even at all stages of this recipe. The sugar can burn quite quickly when unattended or too hot. Dry on parchment and store in airtight container.

Cinnamon Spice Cookies
Soft, spiced cookies
preheat oven to 350°F
makes 36

1 cup butter
1 cup sugar
2 eggs
2 cups unbleached flour
2 cups regular oats
1 tsp baking powder
½ tsp baking soda
¼ tsp salt
2 tsp cinnamon
¼ cup milk
1 cup chopped apple
½ cup raisins (optional)

Method

Beat butter and sugar together in bowl. Add eggs and beat till fluffy.

In second bowl, combine flour, oats, baking powder, baking soda, salt and cinnamon. Mix well. Add apple chunks. Alternate dry ingredients into wet adding the milk between.

Grease cookie sheet. Drop by tablespoons onto sheet. Leave room between for cookies to double in size. Bake for 10-12 minutes. Ovens vary, so adjust time accordingly.

Serve with a piping-hot cup of coffee.

French Pancakes
buttery and rich
thin pancakes
preheat frying pan
makes 4

1 cup unbleached flour
1/2 tsp salt
1-1/2 cup milk
3 eggs, well beaten

Method

Sift flour and salt together. Add milk and beaten eggs. Batter should be as thick as heavy cream. Butter the frying pan, pour in a little batter, tilt pan back and forth to allow batter to cover bottom; when brown, flip over and brown other side. Spread with butter and jam, fruit or syrup. Roll and sprinkle with icing sugar. Serve hot.

Cool Idea

Do you have a collection of favorite family recipes handed down from generations of cooks but they are in ten different recipe books? Why not create your own family heirloom recipe book? To be able to hand down a book of classic family recipe is such a wonderful legacy. To get started, buy a blank, lined book or use your creativity to make your own recipe collection with lined paper and a binder.

You can also buy recipe cards and a box. Create beautiful pages with your own art or use a computer to do all the typing and graphics. Make it as embellished or as plain as you like. This is something you may want to hand down to your child, so it should be put together well and be able to stand the test of time. I still have a Duo-Tang that my mom made me when I was a teen. She filled it with recipes and quotes and hand-drawn images to go along with the quotes. I cherish it. It is a pretty special book.

Interesting Stuff

Did you know there are some foods that have an almost spellbinding and intoxicating scent that may affect your mood in a positive way? Here are some of the more common food scents and what they can do for your mood. There is some scientific evidence showing that when we associate a food scent with a positive outcome, we will use that as a baseline, meaning every time we smell something in particular, it invokes a past emotion. A wonderful scent usually connects to a wonderful memory.

cinnamon	may sharpen the mind, memory and attention span
lemon	may energize the body and promote concentration
vanilla	may improve your mood by elevating joy and relaxed feelings
lavender	may calm the body and aid in good sleep
pine	may decrease anxiety
peppermint	may boost concentration and calm the body before bed.

Do you use oils or aroma to change your mood? If so, which ones?

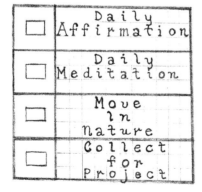

SHANNON BRAYBROOK

I sure hope you have enjoyed spending time nourishing your mind, body and soul.
I enjoyed creating this little book for you.
My wish for you is a life of peaceful happiness and joy.
Namaste.

Lightning Source UK Ltd.
Milton Keynes UK
UKHW032153260620
365625UK00008B/692